THE EDUCATOR'S ENIGMA:

The Adolescent with Learning Disabilities

Edited by Ellen Schloss

President
Fund for Perceptually Handicapped Children
Evanston, Illinois

Academic Therapy Publications
San Rafael, California

Library of Congress Catalog Card Number: 76-157140
ISBN Number: 0-87879-021-7

Printed in the United States of America
2nd printing 1972

This book is based on papers delivered at a seminar entitled "Educator's Engima: The Adolescent with Learning Disabilities," presented by the Fund for Perceptually Handicapped Children, Inc., Box 656, Evanston, Illinois, with the assistance of the North Shore Service League, held at Deerfield, Illinois, March 2, 1968.

CONTENTS

Foreword

I T IS A PRIVILEGE to write this foreword for a book that will
stand as a memorial to Howard Lurie. For many years, Bud, as
he was known to his friends, symbolized in action the commitment
of parents who work with handicapped children. Rarely does one
know a man who is able to combine ideas and action into con-
structive help for others. Bud Lurie was one such man. His un-
timely death in April, 1970 closed a chapter in the history of the
Fund for Perceptually Handicapped Children. It was primarily
through his efforts that the seminar — from which the papers in
this book emerged — made a major contribution in bringing together
parents, professionals of many disciplines, and nationally recog-
workers in the field. This seminar focused on the adolescent with
learning problems.

Through the past ten years it had become increasingly clear
that teachers and administrators of older children with learning
problems had little awareness and few of the skills needed to be
helpful to such children. Moreover, the normal problems of adolescence added complications to the task of understanding these
children. It was therefore a timely venture that this seminar was
directed to teachers and educators responsible for the education
of adolescents.

If the reader is challenged by the material in these papers,
the authors will be gratified.

Mary Giffin, M.D.

Who Is He?

Charles R. Strother, Ph.D.

SO MUCH HAS been said and written about the subject of learning disabilities that it is difficult to discuss it without covering familiar ground. At least three main groups are aware of this problem. One group is composed of parents – and parents who recognize the problem of learning disabilities are very sophisticated. They have read the literature; they are familiar with the concepts and the controversies in the field. There is a second group composed of professionals and university graduate students entering the fields of psychology and special education who are also quite sophisticated in their knowledge of the literature. I am not going to direct my comments, however, to either of these groups. The primary purpose of this paper is to convey some information to the junior high and high school teachers, both the general classroom teachers and the special education teachers at these levels.

There has been so much emphasis on the early diagnosis and treatment of children with learning disabilities that the problems of the adolescent have been seriously neglected. Everyone approves of the emphasis on early diagnosis and treatment. There is no question that a great deal more can be accomplished if the child is identified at an early age and a remedial program is initiated as soon as possible. In fact, the attempt nowadays is to move diagnosis and the beginning of training down as close as possible to the day of birth. There are a number of experimental programs being developed that start with a child who is a few weeks of age.

PROBLEMS IN DEFINING LEARNING DISABILITIES

Who is the child with learning disabilities? Is he the child with minimal brain damage? Is he the child with psychoneurological learning disabilities? Is he the child with minimal cerebral dysfunction? Is he the child with perceptual handicaps? Is he the child with dyslexia? Are these terms synonymous, or do they refer to different children? If so, do these different children all belong under the rubric of *the child with learning disabilities?* With this amount of technological confusion in the literature, it is not surprising that parents, teachers, and professionals are confused. I like the title of the major address that Dr. Samuel A. Kirk gave to an international meeting two or three years ago, which was simply, "We are all Confused." In this paper I will attempt to clear away some of this confusion, recognizing that it is a task to which I am not equal. But such an attempt must be made, and I am going to do so very dogmatically. I am going to express my own opinion and the reader may take it for whatever he feels it may be worth.

Disagreement on Etiology

Confusion arises from a variety of sources. First, a difference of opinion exists as to the etiology of these learning disorders, and here there are three particular groups. One group maintains that these learning disabilities represent a dysfunction that is of genetic, or traumatic, or developmental origin. Those who hold this position will admit that sometimes neurological examination can demonstrate a dysfunction of the central nervous system with sufficient clarity so that there is little disagreement among competent neurologists as to the existence of pathology. They will admit, on the other hand, that in a considerable number of cases the neurological symptoms are only suggestive, only warrant raising a suspicion of a central nervous system dysfunction. Even the most conservative of them will admit that in a considerable proportion of cases the neurological pathology has to be simply inferred. There is no neurological evidence that can be agreed upon by competent experts in these cases, and the diagnosis is strictly an inferential diagnosis. This represents one point of view.

There is a second group that maintains that the evidence of central nervous system *pathology,* even where it exists, is not sufficiently clear cut to warrant the assumption that there is an underlying central nervous system *disability,* and that to use terms that imply a central nervous system disability is thus not warranted. There is a third group that maintains that a presumed or an established central nervous system etiology is of no importance because it doesn't help in working with the child. There is no kind of surgery, there is no kind of medication, there is no kind of physiotherapy, there is no form of medical treatment that will be of substantial assistance in dealing with the learning disabilities of the child.

There are, then, these three points of view with respect to etiology. I agree with the second of these positions. I also agree with the third. I think the second and third positions are compatible. I don't believe that the neurological diagnosis is helpful in treatment. I believe that it is harmful to the child to imply a central nervous system pathology. The appropriate point of view for an educator to take is that he is concerned with the learning disabilities and what can be done with them through education. Others may choose to take a different position. Many of my friends, particularly many of my neurological friends, choose to do so. But a choice must be made. I would like to interject that I am anxious to find a group of neurologists who will take the following bet. Take a representative sample of these children, get detailed neurological data on them, present that detailed neurological data to five equally competent neurologists, and determine the extent to which they can agree with each other on which children they classify as neurologically damaged and which children they classify as without neurological damage. What I am implying is that the unreliability of neurological diagnosis is very high, and this is one thing that is often ignored in evaluating this kind of approach, this kind of evidence. So one source of confusion lies in a difference of opinion as to the etiology.

Diversity of Symptoms

A second source of confusion arises from the many symptoms that are found in a group of children who are loosely termed children with learning disabilities, or specific learning disabilities. Some of the terminology that is applied, particularly *perceptually handicapped,* or *dyslexic,* or comparable terms, focus attention on a specific kind of learning problem. There is no great difference of opinion that these specific kinds of learning disabilities do exist and constitute primary and major problems in the child's learning. However, none of these terms encompasses the full scope of the problems that are presented by children with specific learning disabilities. Among this group of children are those with difficulties in auditory or visual perception; with problems of memory, short term and long term memory; with problems of information processing, concept formation, and problem solving; and with problems of oral and written expression. There has been a vigorous search for syndromes, for combinations of these problems. But the research that I am familiar with has generally concluded that the diagnosis must be on an individual basis, that while generally there are children whose major problems fall in one or another of these aspects of cognitive functioning, nevertheless the individual differences are sufficiently great to require individual rather than categorical treatment. There is, then, no disagreement on the existence of a diversity of special learning disabilities, or on the need to use different materials and different approaches when they relate to the problems presented by the particular child.

Ambiguity in Research

I don't believe, however, that the search for some kind of a definition of a learning disability can be given up. A definition — an explicit definition — is important from the standpoint of research. In the research literature there is a great deal of ambiguity, a great deal of discrepancy in the results. These discrepancies come largely from the fact that two researchers dealing with the same procedures have dealt with different populations of children, and therefore their results are quite different. This has led to a tremendous amount of confusion in the research literature, which is regrettable. I have made this point many times, and I would like to make it again, particularly for those who are going to present research papers to professional audiences: it is the responsibility of the professional to define explicitly the criteria for the selection of the population with which he is doing research. Unless that population is defined explicitly and in operational terms, it is impossible to evaluate the data and the inferences that are drawn from the data.

IT IS IMPORTANT, for educational purposes, to arrive at a definition of a learning disability. When an attempt is made to set up special facilities and special educational procedures for these children, specific criteria must be established for admissions eligibility and for the

6

kinds of programs that will be provided. The problem is particularly acute in those states where there is state aid for special education — where the state is prepared, as it is in my state, Washington, to pay up to a maximum of $1,800 for every child who is admitted to a special education class. When a special education class for children with learning disabilities is set up, it is the tendency of the bright school administrator who knows he will get $1,800 extra for every child he puts into that class, to crowd into it all of the children who are having any kind of a problem. I would do the same thing if I were a school superintendent and had a great need of funds. (What school superintendent doesn't nowadays?) This is, of course, something that has to be controlled. To control it, there must be a fairly explicit definition of who is eligible for admission to special classes for children with learning disabilities. It is an unnecessary expense and delay to require that a neurologist conduct an examination of the child and be willing to sign a statement saying that the child has minimal brain dysfunction or central nervous system disability of some sort. This puts a neurologist in an ethical conflict that is unfair to him and is a waste of the rare medical resources in this field.

A DEFINITION OF LEARNING DISABILITIES

There have been a number of rather high-level official attempts to arrive at a definition of learning disabilities. Probably the most important attempt was launched cooperatively by the National Society of Crippled Children, the National Institute of Neurological Diseases and Blindness, and the Office of Education. Several years ago a meeting was held to bring together all of the federal agencies and all of the private foundations interested in this problem and to decide how to approach a definition of learning disabilities and how to reach some agreement on remedial procedures. The result of this meeting was the setting up of three task forces. The first task force was to concern itself with definition and diagnosis; the second task force was to concern itself with approaches to treatment and training; the third task force was to concern itself with a review of research in this field.

The first task force has published its findings and its recommendations, which do not clarify the situation very much. They simply conclude that these children show a diversity of problems and suggest that the best term to use to describe them would be *minimal cerebral dysfunction.* I agree with the first conclusion; I disagree with the second.

7

The second task force is composed of two groups; a medical group and an educational group. The medical committee is concerned with the medical approach to this problem, and the educational committee is concerned with an educational approach. When these reports come out, the reader may take his choice. If he reads both of them, he will become confused. He should read one and draw some security from whatever it has to say.

The third task force, of which I am a member, is concerning itself with a review of research; one of the principal conclusions that we will draw is that the research is very confused. I agree with that conclusion! This ambitious attempt is under way and is about to be concluded and the hope is that once the third task force has submitted its report, there will be a big national conference and this conference will decide just how we are going to define, diagnose and treat learning disabilities. I suppose the conference will be held, and I suppose if it is held I will attend, but I am not very optimistic about the possibility of reaching any conclusions. I stated earlier, however, that it is necessary to arrive at *some* definition.

One group that has a responsibility for such a definition is a committee that was set up recently by congressional action. There has been a great deal of controversy on the national level in the Congress and in the Office of Education about how programs for the education of the handicapped are to be administered. These programs were, for a time, dispersed throughout the Office of Education in a division of elementary and secondary education, a division of research, and so on. There was a good deal of feeling on the part of organizations like the Fund for Perceptually Handicapped Children and many other politically powerful organizations that the problems of the handicapped were being neglected, and that the work for the handicapped needed to be drawn together in a specific unit of the Office of Education. So the Bureau for the Education of the Handicapped was set up by congressional action. Dr. James Gallagher was appointed Director of that Bureau, and the Congress established an Advisory Committee on the Education of the Handicapped. This committee then had to formulate a definition of learning disabilities that could be used for the allocation of federal funds, so that universities applying for funds for support of students wanting training in this field could be identified as being eligible for funds under this particular category. This committee has arrived at a definition, and I am sorry that it has not been more widely publicized. It is the definition on which the Office of Education is now basing its allocation of funds, and it is going to have a considerable influence on the definitions that are utilized in the states. The definition is as follows:

> Children with special learning disabilities exhibit a disorder in one or more of the basic psychological processes involved in understanding or using spoken or written language. These may be manifested in disorders of listening, thinking, talking, reading, writing, spelling, or arithmetic. They include conditions which have been referred to as perceptual handicaps, brain injuries, minimal brain dysfunction, dyslexia, developmental aphasia. They do not include learning problems which are due primarily to visual, hearing or motor handicaps, to mental retardation, emotional disturbance, or to environmental disadvantage.

THIS DEFINITION can be useful in making an attempt to locate the child with learning disabilities, but there are special problems in identifying these children on the secondary level. Identification may be easier on the elementary school level than it is on the secondary level. The reason for this is that with a young child, simply the primary learning disability is evident. The child hasn't yet been defeated by his learning disability. But by the time this child arrives at the junior high school or the high school level, he has had many years of persistent confusion and persistent frustration to which he has reacted in a variety of ways.

At the junior high or high school level there is a tremendous overlay related to this primary learning disability, and this confuses the picture. This makes it more difficult to discriminate between the child with a primary learning disability and the child who is emotionally disturbed, or the child who is a behavior problem because he is acting out. The long duration of his learning disability and the experiences he has had as the consequence of this disability may affect his motivation, his interest in school, and his desire to attempt to learn. He may appear to be a child who is indifferent or resistant to learning. His learning difficulties may have resulted in a great deal of anxiety and all kinds of defense mechanisms against the anxiety, so that he may look like a very neurotic child. It may have resulted, and it does frequently in the brighter children, in his having found some way of circumventing this difficulty, some individual or peculiar way of accomplishing a task, which looks bizarre but which is effective for him, and this confuses the issue. He may have adopted a lot of compensatory or reactive acting out behavior that also serves to confuse the picture. So it is more difficult on the junior high and high school level to identify the child with primary learning disabilities.

BEHAVIOR

What are some of the things that the secondary school teacher can see that may lead him to suspect that the child whom he is observing may be a child with special learning disabilities? Because these symptoms can be complex, it is helpful for the teacher to have some simple way to organize his thoughts about behavior – some simple way of looking at a child and asking the question, "Does his difficulty fall in this, that, or the other particular area?" My answer to this question is not a unique idea. It is repeated in the literature and incorporated in many batteries of diagnostic tests. There are four major categories of disturbance, four major aspects of behavior, which the teacher may find useful in his observation of children with special learning disabilities. These children are often found in one or another of the categories.

Visual and Auditory Problems

Chronologically, the first aspect of an act of behavior is taking in information from the environment, primarily through the eyes and through the ears. Although information comes through in other ways, these are the most important avenues for concept development and concept formation. Some of these children have difficulty in structuring what they hear or what they see. By structuring, I simply mean telling the difference between two different combinations of sounds, or the difference between two different letters. For example, the inability to tell the difference between the words *man* and *moon* is the kind of perceptual difficulty that many of these children have. Children who have this type of difficulty show a great deal of misunderstanding of what is said, sometimes very bizarre and particular misunderstandings. Many things are understood, but many things are misunderstood. It is difficult, unless there is careful observation, to make sense out of this inconsistency in understanding. These children may also have a difficulty in visual input so that they misread words or are unable to distinguish the difference between the words — for example, the word *they* and the word *boy* — when these are seen on the printed page. Sometimes these difficulties in misreading words are very unusual, and in some cases these children, of course, can't read at all. But by the time children have reached the junior high level, most of them have acquired some limited degree of reading ability.

Hyperactivity

There is a second group of children who are generally hyperactive and who have difficulties in attention and retention, who may need to have directions repeated several times before they can remember them even briefly, who may have a rapid rate of forgetting, and consequently need a great deal of spaced repetition before information can be retained. These children present a special kind of problem.

Conceptualization Problems

After information is taken in and retained, it must be processed in some way to develop concepts. The information must be used in operations like problem solving, and the children in this third group often have difficulties with this kind of thinking process. The classical kind of conceptual problem is of course the problem of concreteness, a difficulty in understanding abstract ideas. This often expresses itself in more or less amusing ways in the misinterpretation of figures of speech.

For a period of four or five years I was responsible for a group of adolescent children with learning disabilities for whom we felt social training was very important. Twice a week these children were taken in small groups to different restaurants so that they would become familiar with social behavior in a restaurant situation, familiar with ordering food, and familiar with the arithmetic involved in calculating the check. One of the boys who had this particular kind of difficulty in thinking exhibited it in two delightful illustrations. The teacher and the group were talking in the restaurant and this boy had talked a little too much, which he usually did, so the

teacher said to him, "John, I'm fed up with your argument." His answer was, "If you're fed up, may I have the rest of your sandwich?"
On another occasion they were getting ready to leave, and the
teacher said, "Who will foot the bill?" John picked up the bill and
threw it on the floor and said, "I'll foot it, but why?" This is typi-
cal of the difficulty in abstract thinking that many of these children
have, and it produces some very peculiar social and linguistic behavior.

Speech and Writing Problems

Once information has been taken in, registered, and processed,
some kind of output must occur; a response must be made in the form
of speech or writing. Thus, we come to the fourth group of children.
They show many disorders in their writing: severe spelling problems;
grammatical disorders; and all forms of difficulty with syntax. They
also manifest many confusions and impoverishments of verbal output
and difficulties with spatial perception. This is especially true in
the case of those children who cannot tell how to get to one particular place and who cannot judge distances.

THESE ARE THE KINDS of problems that the secondary school
teacher will see as evidences of learning disabilities, and they
are overlaid by a variety of other problems. The classroom teacher
and the special teacher are not — certainly for children on the secondary level — to be expected to accomplish a differential diagnosis.
The problem is too complicated. Therefore, there must be some kind
of an assessment procedure by means of which children who have
been suspected of belonging to this group, on the basis of symptoms
such as those described, can be referred for a differential diagnosis
and for an educational prescription. This is the responsibility of a
special resource in a school system, and it cannot be dispensed with
if the school is concerned about dealing with these children efficiently.

How Do We Find Him?

Rosa A. Hagin, Ph.D.

HOW DOES THE ADOLESCENT with a learning disability look to the people who are responsible for his care? How does he look to the people in his school, to the secondary school teacher who is to teach him (along with approximately 119 others), to the counselor who will advise him and discuss his post-high-school training, to the vice-principal who may have to deal with his behavior problems, to the clinician to whom he might be referred?

In the secondary school, the adolescent is experiencing his most trying time. Added to the normative adolescent turmoil is, first of all, a major cognitive defect: pervasive inadequacy in dealing with symbols. This inadequacy may show up in various ways. It may show up in difficulty in learning chemical symbols or the phylla in biology, in left-right orientation as he learns to drive. The adolescent with a learning disability may have trouble listening in school. He may find that he becomes so lost in the teacher's words that he cannot take notes fast enough during lectures and discussions. He may experience overwhelming anxiety with examinations. Although he works hard, he may find that others, not any brighter than he, receive better marks on compositions and recitations because of their easy verbalization or free-flowing pens. Underlying all these problems, the adolescent may feel the nagging fear that he might not, after all, be very bright. At the secondary level, the teacher represents a sensitive area in this youngster's feelings. The school is where he has failed in the past, and teachers keep telling him he could do better. During the teen years, life becomes real. Work at school is important, not just to please parents and teachers, but because this youngster realizes his life goals depend upon literacy.

At adolescence a learning disability is not a matter of achieving or failing to achieve at school. At this time he is experiencing the complex interplay of capacities and deficits, of psychological defenses and environmental supports. In short, at adolescence we see the progress and the scars of all that has been done to and for the child with a learning disability.

Maturation may obscure some of the perceptual deficits that might have been easily recognized when he was six or seven years of age. For example, by age fifteen he may have learned to control the tremor by constriction or to mask it by clowning. He may handle left-right discrimination by cues such as the watch on the arm or the freckle on the hand. He begins to use other kinds of compensations as well, some of them healthy, some of them less so. He may develop specialities, all-consuming interests such as photography, art, athletics, and mathematics. He may become aggressive and adopt the posture of the "hood." On the other hand, he may go in the direction of withdrawal, starting with nonattendance, going on to truancy or dropping out of school. He may try psychological withdrawal by taking refuge in drugs and hallucinogens. His defenses may take the form of denial, the putting on of a hard, shiny surface that maintains that "spelling is unimportant, who needs it?" Or he may somaticize his problems with vague physical ailments that keep him out of school. All of these are examples of behaviors that teachers see in the secondary school. It is necessary to look beneath this overlay in order to understand the basic syndrome of specific language disability.

THE SYNDROME of specific language disability is a discrepancy between expectancy and achievement in the use, comprehension, and written expression of ideas. Adolescents with specific language disability have difficulty with one or more of the language arts: listening, speaking, reading, and writing — either handwriting or composition. These difficulties occur despite intact senses, adequate intelligence, conventional instruction, and normal motivation.

14

When these children are examined with psychological, neurological, and perceptual tests, the following characteristics are found:

- Lack of neurological organization corresponding to cerebral dominance for language as seen in defects in right-left discrimination; discrepancy between preferred hand and elevated arm on an extension test; postural responses less mature and less well organized than might be expected of a youngster of the patient's age on a neurological examination.
- Visual-motor difficulties, including problems in spatial orientation and in separation of figure from background.
- Auditory problems, with specific difficulties in discrimination and ordering the temporal relationship of sounds.
- Body image problems, as seen particularly in tonus and postural problems and in indications of finger agnosia.
- Tactile figure-background problems.

Nine out of ten of the children seen in our Language Research Unit (New York University School of Medicine) demonstrate some, but not necessarily all, of these problems. Two out of these nine show, in addition, signs that suggest to the neurologist structural damage to the central nervous system. Therefore, three groups may be defined: (1) the seven out of ten of the retarded readers who have developmental defects described in the basic syndrome; (2) the two out of ten who have, in addition, signs of central nervous system dysfunction; and (3) the remaining one who is relatively free of perceptual or neurological problems but has an emotionally based learning disability. This last group represents a different etiology from that which I have discussed. Diagnosis and evaluation of assets and deficits is important because etiology frequently determines prognosis and because diagnostic information enables us to select appropriate teaching approaches.

HOW DOES ONE LOCATE and differentiate the child with specific language disability at the secondary level? My experience leads me to conclude that careful, individual, clinical diagnosis is necessary. It is important not only to be able to evaluate the response itself, but also the process by which the response was made. Observations made by experienced teachers and concerned parents are also a rewarding source of data. Observations of the following characteristics are helpful:

- Highs and lows in functioning.
- Methods by which the child handles language: the content, possible word-finding difficulties, spoonerisms, auditory discrimination difficulties, sequencing, and left-right discrimination.
- Handwriting, with particular emphasis on the way the youngster grips the pencil.
- Approaches to the task of reading. (How does he attack words? How does he deal with factual comprehension, with interpretation, with study skills? What is his rate of reading?)
- Spelling methods.
- Difficulties he has had with other kinds of symbols such as Morse Code and shorthand.
- Observations of his spatial abilities made by the industrial arts teacher or fine arts teacher.

Careful clinical evaluation needs supportive information concerning the child's developmental history, his neurological functioning, his psychiatric status, his psychological and perceptual abilities, and his educational skills. With information like this, reasonable planning can be provided for the child. Etiology influences prognosis as well as helps to determine plans for reteaching. These diagnostic methods have been described elsewhere in detail.[1] Instead of describing them here, I would like to illustrate from longitudinal case records that were collected during follow-up studies on three of the children with specific language disability whom I have watched grow up.[2] These children, not necessarily the textbook cases, show some of the perils the child with a reading disability faces as an adolescent. The first was a youngster from the group with organic reading disabilities (those who show signs of central nervous system dysfunction).

Lenny was referred to our medical center because of a facial tic and behavior difficulties. There were neurological findings that were minor, but present, on neurological examination. There were also perceptual problems in the visual, auditory and tactile modalities. Lenny's reading was characterized by poor comprehension, inadequate phrasing, and a slow rate. Indeed, he was so preoccupied with word-analysis skills that the meaning of what he read was all but lost. As a ten-year-old, Lenny entered our remedial reading program. He responded well during the year and one-half that we worked with him. However, when he reached junior high school, his school work fell off. I didn't see Lenny again until he was twenty years of age. At that time he had dropped from a public high school during the seventh term. He had become discouraged when he was unable to pass English, and he found himself repeating the subject, semester after semester. He was disappointed because he had failed to graduate, and he found his poor reading skills to be a vocational handicap. At the time of follow-up he was employed in semiskilled jobs. It was his ambition to complete high school requirements if he could qualify for military service. On follow-up study, his oral reading scored within the ninth grade level, his comprehension at the sixth percentile on the Survey Section of the *Diagnostic Reading Test.*[3] His reading continued to be slow, with a rate of 156 words per minute.

A more optimistic picture comes with *Virginia,* who represents the child with a developmental reading disability. She has the problems that I described in the basic syndrome, but on neurological examination there was no evidence, as there was with Lenny, of structural defect of the central nervous system.

Virginia came to the clinic with complaints of difficulty in learning to read and spell. Her achievement test scores were at the second grade level, despite placement in grade six at school and average intelligence. Her mother was concerned because her daughter was dependent upon her, experienced night terrors and some sleepwalking. The mother, an observant young woman, said sadly, "She was a good child until she went to school."

Despite being a gently reared youngster, Virginia quarrelled with nearly everyone at school. Even the gym teacher became the object of her wrath during a lesson on square dancing when "grand right and left" confused her unstable directionality. As far as her reading was concerned, Virginia was at a loss for independent word-attack skills. Her reading difficulty resulted not from lack of understanding, but from inability to decode the symbols. She moved rapidly with the tutoring, and her progress continued even after tutoring was terminated. On follow-up study, she reported completion of a commercial course at high school. Her oral reading scored at the eleventh grade level and her comprehension at the twenty-fourth percentile, but her spelling lagged behind at the seventh grade level. She was working as a receptionist and secretary. I imagine that she made good use of the dictionary in transcribing letters. She said she worried sometimes when her employer asked her to compose letters on her own. She wondered whether the sentences sounded simple and childish. She said she'd had some difficulty in learning shorthand, which is a very interesting aspect of the symbolization problem. Emotionally, she had come through her childhood difficulties and was looking forward confidently to adult responsibilities.

Some children considerably more disabled than Lenny or Virginia were also included in our program, even though we felt a more guarded prognosis was indicated for them. On follow-up we were, in some cases, surprised by the long-term results. Lauretta Bender has pointed out the lags in development that characterize some children with serious emotional problems.[4] These lags may be seen in the way some of them learn language skills. A number of children whom we have studied in the years at Bellevue hospital have shown perceptual and neurological characteristics not unlike the developmental reading disability group. It was interesting on follow-up to discover that the plasticity that characterizes this group worked to their advantage in the improvement of language skills; on the other hand, their thinking disturbances led to problems in comprehension that are not usually seen with the developmental language disability.

Ten-year-old *Sam* was referred to the mental hygiene clinic by the medical social worker on a pediatrics ward where he had attracted attention by his difficulties with other children. He'd been hospitalized for an adenoidectomy. It soon was apparent that he talked to himself, entertained imaginary playmates, and refused to accept his mother as his real parent. The school had considered him a dull child and had placed him in classes for children with retarded mental development. Intellectual functioning was borderline with an IQ of 81 earned on the revised *Stanford-Binet Intelligence Scale*. There was some scatter in scoring, but abilities seemed generally limited. Neurologically he was intact, except for some of the soft signs which have been associated with reading disability. He had a normal electroencephalogram. Right-left discrimination, however, was confused. He knew the alphabet by rote, but he was unable to read anything else. He regarded this as "my secret," and he tried to keep this information from others. After two and one-half years of tutoring, his oral reading score rose to the fourth grade level, although comprehension was less advanced, placing at the third grade level. When Sam returned for follow-up study, he had completed fifty units at one of the community colleges. Most surprising of all, his intellectual functioning on the *Wechsler Adult Intelligence Scale* was within the bright-average range, with an IQ of 117 earned on formal testing. What happened in the interval? The transcript of his follow-up interview answers this question in Sam's own words:

> Well, I've been going to a community college in the evening, and I am working during the day as a stock clerk in a store. And once every month I go down to the naval field for a reserve meeting. And within six months I should be far away from here.
>
> *Where will you be in six months?*
> On a ship, I guess, somewhere.
> *Oh, actually on sea duty. What will you be doing on the ship?*
> Well, I'm striving to be a mechanic, but they want to put me in an office because of my score on an exam; I was high in filing. But I don't want to go in the navy and be in an office.
> *You want to run the ship, eh? What are you studying at college?*
> Business administration.
> *What subjects are you taking there?*
> I am taking history, Medieval History, and I am learning an awful lot by it. It teaches you more of why things are the way they are now. And then I'm taking business courses.
> *You must do a lot of reading.*
> I do a comparative amount. I don't do that much reading. I really should do more. I'm very lazy, very lazy.
> *Tell me what you did after I finished seeing you, as far as school is concerned.*
> Six months after I saw you they gave me an examination and they decided I was a qualified student for the regular class. And then they put me in the sixth grade. And I'll never forget, before they put me in the sixth grade, this incident when the teacher put me way in front of her, and I felt so terribly funny that day. And the next day she told me that I was to be transfered to a sixth grade. And then I went to high school. And I did rather well in my first year in high school. I had the highest average in my class which was about a ninety. When I went to occupational high school, they noted I didn't have a very high quotient on my aptitude test so they wanted to put me in nonacademic courses. So I had a kind of a high average

on my math and the teacher who was in charge of math noticed
that I had a high score on my exams that they gave me when
I came in to the school. And he said, "You don't belong in
this class," so I went down to the guidance teacher and she
seen that the teacher recommended me for a regular math
class, so she said, "Oh well, why don't I put you in a regular
'bio' class too," and so she did. So the next year for some
strange reason – I guess I did the teacher a favor or something
– so she thought I appeared rather bright and so she recommended me for an honors math class. So I spent six months in a
speeded up math course. And later on I found out that in an
academic high school this was equal to a regular class. Then
I was also put in an honors history class later on. I never
know how I did it (laughs).

I'll bet you're pleased with yourself about this.

Yes, and I passed all my science. I took four years of science in high school. I was very surprised when I passed the
English Regents. I never thought I'd pass it because of my
background, you know. It made me feel good, especially
when one of my friends didn't pass it.

What was hard for you in high school?

My hardest subject was French.

Did you pass that or drop it?

Well, you see, I'm a very persistent person.

I remember that.

It took a few times and she finally passed me. There's one
thing I seem to have a mental block for, that's language.

Have you tried any other language since then?

No, I haven't.

*What do you think made the difference for you as far as get-
ting along in school is concerned?*

There's so many things. Well, one of the things was that
the better I did in school the more acceptable I became to my
friends, in my eyes . . . (long hesitation). . . and my family
treated me with more respect and made me feel more like I
was an average individual, which I always wanted to be. I always recall the first day I went to the CRMD (Children of Retarded Mental Development) class. I cried. Maybe for two days
or so. And I always felt that nobody else had anything in common with me so I didn't bother with anyone. As if they were of
a better background, better race.

How do you feel about this now?

I still do. I had this feeling of trying to prove myself.
That's why I'm always pushing myself, but I don't know if it's
good or not, but I can't stop. One thing, I just can't stand

still, you know, and I decided that this term I wanted to take something different. So I decided to take a course at visual arts school.

So you're taking that as well as working and going to college and going to the naval reserve. That's quite a schedule.

Yes.

What will come next after you've served your term in the navy? What do you see ahead?

I'd like to buy myself a little house. I don't know about getting married. I don't feel adequate in that way. I'd like to try to make money through my own wits, you know. I'd like to buy a house with land on it, divide the acreage and build houses on it. I'd get loans on the house I have and build more houses. I'd put back the money I got for the first house and build a second house. I hear of people becoming very prosperous that way. That's just an idea, and I'll always go to school. It's something I have to do.

This boy still has problems, as his frank and insightful response indicates. We should not mislead ourselves into believing that the emotional disturbance of his childhood has been cured; however, the academic skills that he obtained have given him a "handle on the world" and have made the difference in his ego development. I believe that the hospitable reactions of the teachers in his schools were to a large measure responsible for the acquisition of these academic skills.

SPECIFIC LANGUAGE DISABILITY has been described as a complex of neurological, psychiatric, psychological, perceptual, and educational behaviors. At adolescence these youngsters are seen at their most difficult time, for there is an interplay of constitutional factors, of developing psychological needs and defenses, and of external pressures and supports. Locating, diagnosing, and teaching them require systematic observations and objectivity gained from a familiarity with normal development. It also requires patience. Teaching, which has its foundation in careful, multidisciplinary diagnosis, is important to the realization of the child's potential abilities. Our follow-up studies have made us optimistic about these youngsters when teaching has been appropriate. We are grateful to have known these youngsters, not so much for what we have taught them, but for what they have taught us.

NOTES

1. A. A. Silver and R. A. Hagin, "Specific Reading Disability: An Approach to Diagnosis and Treatment," *Journal of Special Education,* I (Winter 1967), 109-118.
2. A. A. Silver and R. A. Hagin, "Specific Reading Disability: Follow-up Studies," *American Journal of Orthopsychiatry,* XXXIV (1964), 95-102.
3. For sources of tests mentioned in this article, see references.
4. L. Bender, "Problems in Conceptualization and Communication in Children with Developmental Alexia," *Psychopathology of Communication,* eds. P. Hoch and J. Zubin (New York, N.Y.: Grune & Stratton, 1958).

REFERENCES

Terman, E. Lewis, and Maud A. Merrill. *Stanford-Binet Intelligence Scale.* Boston, Mass.: Houghton-Mifflin, 1962 (revised).

Triggs, Frances O., and others. *Diagnostic Reading Test.* Mt. Home, N.C.: Committee on Diagnostic Reading Tests, Inc., 1966.

Wechsler, David I. *Wechsler Adult Intelligence Scale.* New York, N.Y.: Psychological Corporation, 1955.

How Does He Feel?

Mary Giffin, M.D.

PSYCHIATRISTS REALLY DO NOT contribute much to this field. We simply learn from the teachers and other educators who work with learning-disabled children how to avoid the mistakes we made in the past when we assumed that all children with learning disabilities were emotionally conflicted. Perhaps there are some observations, however, that I can mention that will prove helpful in understanding these children.

During the last four months I have been trying to help a friend die. This is one of the growing experiences of psychiatry. It is now known that each stress of life is a developmental phase. Many psychiatrists have become interested in helping individuals experience the dignity of death, rather than the loneliness of dying. My friend is one of the greatest preachers in this country. He was a Jeremiah. He has been transformed into a Job. He was a silver-tongued orator, a pungent writer, and a positive actionist whose every move reflected values. This man had an inoperable brain tumor of his language area. One day in writing an important article, he thought he knew what he was writing, but when his wife read the article, it was jargon. We now must communicate without the assistance of words. I have known him for a long while, and we can now communicate visually, by osmosis, by touch of the hand. It is not difficult to empathize with this man, but what about the feelings of the child who has a language problem, who does not even know what the experience of verbal relatedness is, who does not know that there is such a thing as real verbal communication?

Consider the problem of trying to help a blind person – who has once known vision – to adjust. He has the advantage over many learning-disabled children in the sense that he can be taught to "see" by using some aspect of his previous visual experience. For example, his memory of the image of a clock face can be used to help him "see" the food on his plate: the meat is at "twelve o'clock," the potatoes are at "three o'clock." Empathy is felt for this person also. Somehow, in spite of his affliction, there will be ongoing communication to the best of his ability and the ability of those who try to help him. But what about the child with a visual-perceptual problem who has not known and still may not know that he has an organic difficulty? How do we get inside of his skin so that we can help by sharing his feelings with him? There is an old Ojibway saying that "You should not judge a man until you have walked two moons in his moccasins." This is the problem we have in relating to anyone, but especially in trying to understand the learning disabilities child, who is, in a sense, without language and without sight. My friend in the hospital was able, before he became totally aphasic, to blurt out to his wife, "Honey, I am nothing!" The child with learning disabilities rarely can say it, but he always feels it.

I was reminded recently, when I was talking to a youth group, a group of adolescents, how general is the notion that mentally retarded children and those with learning disabilities do not recognize and do not feel their disabilities. One of the girls in the group brought up the subject by commenting, "Isn't it wonderful that the retarded really don't realize." The next week we went to a special class, which was ironically called "The Happy Club," to observe these children, and it became quickly apparent that these children knew what those who work with them know, namely that they are different, they are branded; for them, the potter's clay slipped. They have feelings too, and they need special help in handling them.

THERE HAS BEEN CONCERN about all of this for a long while. As far back as 1843, Lordat, who lived in Montpellier, France, wrote a retrospective description of his own illness. If my gifted friend could live, it might have been his description. Lordat wrote, "Whilst retaining the memory of the significance of the words heard, I have lost that of their visible signs. When I wish to glance over the book which I have been reading, I found it impossible to read the title. I shall not speak to you of my despair." This is the despair of the aphasic, of the mentally retarded, and especially the child with learning disabilities.

Aldous Huxley tells the story of a doctor asking a patient in a neurological examination to repeat the following: "It shall be the power of the college to examine or not to examine every licentiate." And the patient responded: "And the bikwa in the teamother of the bieftedoodoo." Now if a person wants to be a Kipling, that's exciting. But if he is stuck with this kind of speech as a means of communication, he is obviously in trouble. And when he sees the confusion in the listener's eyes, yet isn't aware of his personalized jargon, he isn't at all sure what's going on. Donald Pritchley has said, "The dyslexic is apt to find himself alone in a critical if not a hostile milieu, misunderstood or penalized." Should the child be of high intelligence, his prospects of developing neurotic reactions may be greater. As an adolescent, the dyslexic occupies a ridiculous position, unable to read menus, programs, or film titles. He is doomed to second-class citizenship. This is the fate of the children who fall in this wide category of learning disabilities.

As a psychoanalyst I can't refrain from mentioning that the first book Freud wrote was entitled *On Aphasia.* This symbolizes the continuing base from which he operated, namely the physiological base. He would be very happy, if he were alive today, to know that psychiatrists were being represented in the field of learning disabilities. Psychiatrists can at least emphasize the poignancy of feelings and offset the tragic with some optimistic notes. I was delighted to learn recently that Hans Christian Andersen, the Danish fairy tale writer, was dyslexic. Macdonald Critchley refers to Andersen's handwritten description of his visit to Charles Dickens in London, which is an example of a true dyslexic.[1] Isn't it wonderful that with this handicap he could manage to spin immortal yarns? His case is a good example to use in showing that there are creative sides to these children with learning disabilities.

THE PROBLEM of "How do these children feel?" is not easily
defined because it is difficult to obtain proper communication.
There is some kind of solace in the fact that the communications
experts say that there are ten basic media of communication and that
only the last is verbal. But most persons operate as if verbal communication were the main avenue of relating to one another. When we
look for a few moments at the most poignant experiences of our lives,
we will realize that it is the visual sensitivity, the flick of the hand,
the gesture, the humorous interchange that is really meaningful. But
most of the time when we try to help people share feelings, we are
using verbal communication, at least as the bridge. And what hap-
pens when this is tried with a child who has, let's say, a word-selection problem? A good example of a child with this kind of problem is
the adolescent I have been seeing now for some six years. She is a
child who is a good Congregationalist, who talks about her "conver-
sational" church. This is very humorous if the speaker means it. But
if he does not know that he has said the wrong thing, it can be very
devastating. The other day in great seriousness she said to me, "Dr.
Giffin, I have been coming to you for a long while; in your 'adultery'
do you consult somebody?" This ordinarily would provoke a laugh,
yet at the time I couldn't. All I could hear was this child daring to
ask, "Do you also have to seek help?" The humor was hers, but she
did not recognize it.

What about children with auditory difficulties? I have a favorite
youngster who one day said to me after a successful athletic compe-
tition, "I may not be able to *wead* but I sure can wun a wace." Now
this too is humorous, yet if it involved something less clear, she
would be misunderstood. In the world of humor, puns and double-en-
tendres oil social interchange. We can laugh at the story about the
elderly gentleman who asked the buxom lady for a dance. She said,
"Thank you no, I'm all danced out," and he said, "Oh no, just de-
lightfully plump." Humorous if consciously intended — confusing and
isolating if not.

So there are word-selection problems and there are auditory problems. What about the visual problems? Many people have seen the
examples of visual misperception, which are often included in psychology textbooks, such as the vase against the black background,
or the Ishihara charts for color blindness. They are examples of how

visual misperceptions can interfere with communication because the input is misinterpreted or obfuscated. The child with visual misperceptions is in an equally difficult spot because his input automatically destroys his communication. Another kind of difficulty is evidenced by the child with a learning disability that expresses itself as a basic memory deficit. The memory bank is absent. It is as if everything that went in becomes all "quiggles and squires." As e. e. cummings puts it, "We dance our didn'ts and we sing our dids." This kind of subluxated memory and thought is the kind of thing that some of these children have.

In addition to all of these, there are things that are of importance in terms of personality structure – the intrapsychic problems. From a psychiatric point of view, a child with a learning disability is structurally damaged. In the jargon, he has an ego deficit. Whatever would in another child be an autonomous ego function, is, in the learning disability child, a deficiency in speech, language, perception, memory. And of course psychiatrists do not look at these children as getting into difficulty only when they get into school. They have difficulty from the very first time they take in any sensory input. When the infant looks at the nursing mother, he is seeing the mother differently from his normal siblings. When he hears the coos and nursery rhymes, he is hearing them differently. When he begins to try the "no" and the "yes," he hears them and perceives them inconsistently, and so acts and reacts differently.

TEACHERS DO NOT have to be concerned until the child reaches their baliwick. But the parents, the teachers of the preschool era, are dealing with the misperceptions, the feelings, and the ego deficits from the very beginning. The observant parent of one of these children will say, "Yes, there was something different about this child from the beginning." Before we psychiatrists got educated by the teachers and by colleagues who had been working with these children, we assumed that when a parent said that from the beginning this child was different, he was trying to get himself off the hook of feeling guilty. We now know that he was right, that these children are different. These are the children who do not respond to the nursing experience; they do not respond to the usual kinds of home environment; they are hypersensitive or distractable; and they are often hyperkinetic. These children, from the very beginning of their lives, are blunted, obtunded, wound up – in some way deficient in the potential for the building of a strong ego. They have a much harder time developing a personality structure.

Within the child development field we have come to think of the psychic as having both an anatomy and a physiology. For years the focus was on areas of conflicts, on pathology caused by stress during the different developmental levels. However, even more basic is the internal unfolding and structuring of ego capacities, such as accuracy in perception and refinement in reality testing. Undergirding the impact of conflict is the development of the four basic intrapsychic structures, those which we in the jargon call Id, Ego, Super Ego, and Ego Ideal. These are the structures of personality, and insofar as they are handicapped, the individual is automatically in trouble.

So these children are damaged intrapsychically; they are damaged by the interactions that necessarily occur out of their frustration, both with themselves and with their parents, long before they get to the schoolteacher. They are also damaged by the parental need and society's need to deny the presence of difficulty. We are eternal optimists and we fool ourselves; we use rationalization all too often. Someone has said that rationalization is the process by which we can tell ourselves that it is okay to do what we want to do. It is the most commonly used mechanism, as most persons who are involved with these children know. And very often we rationalize the plight of these children and avoid facing what is actually an undeniable reality. This is why it is so exciting to see children diagnosed and treated early. These children psychically have defense mechanisms similar to those of the family. They borrow the sense of denial. They tend, often because they have learned it from their parents, to project onto the school or onto their teacher, and certainly onto the outside world, the reasons for their difficulty. In addition, the children who are capable of doing so develop very obsessive-compulsive kinds of techniques so that they go over and over again a question or answer, checking the details, and in this way they spend a tremendous amount of energy without much to show for it. These children badly need help. They badly need teachers who can clarify reality, who can insist on the presence of whatever problems there are, but who can equally insist on the common endeavor to overcome those problems.

I was talking recently to a child who is in a special education language-disability class. This is a child with a language problem; I can't begin to paraphrase it, but it was a very poignant interchange, because he had learned that I also see a diabetic child with emotional difficulties. He said to me in his jargon, "The boy with diabetes has a problem?" I said, "Yes." He said, "And I have a problem?" I said "Yes." He said, "The boy with diabetes gets shots?" I said "Yes." Then he said, "And I get teachers." I think this says it beautifully. He was figuring out in what way he compared with a child with another disability.

The question often comes up as to whether a child can face the fact of the handicap and still feel normal. I would answer that by saying that he can't face the fact of the handicap and still feel normal, but he can face the fact of the handicap and not feel any worse off than the next child. And we in our setting almost rub the noses of these children into the presence of their handicap.

So the child is faced with the disabling factors of his handicap, and added to all of this, is the impact of adolescence. It has been said that adolescence is a special form of reality, and I think that is the simplest definition there is. Adolescence is a special form of reality. Whenever I think of adolescence I am reminded of the experience I had while listening to a very scholarly presentation by a professor of theology. His presentation could not have been clearer, it could not have been more pointed, and at the end of the session someone got up and asked a question that was so off the focus that this man sort of shook his head and then said, "All I can say in response is, if my head were screwed on backwards, could I see my toes?" This is the way I feel about adolescence. Absolutely everthing is up for grabs. Such terms as *withdrawn, aggressive,* and *defiant* are often used to describe the behavior of the learning disability adolescent. But these descriptions, though true of the handicapped adolescent, are also applicable to any adolescent — any adolescent is withdrawn, is a showoff, is defiant. Adolescence is a special form of reality. Adolescents have body-image problems; they are hypochondriacal; they are depressed; and they are gay. Adolescents are mercurial, variable, variants of personality.

THE NEED FOR UNDERSTANDING the process of adolescence is vital for the forthcoming years. Fifty percent of the United States population will soon be under the age of twenty-five; half of our population will be struggling not only with the pressures of outer reality but also with the intrapsychic pressure cooker of adolescence. The National Institute of Mental Health has predicted that during the next decade the rate of young people in hospitals will double, and it is certain that a very large percentage of those people will be learning disability children who have been unrecognized or who have been labeled as schizophrenic because of their queer conceptual difficulties; they will continue to go unrecognized.

An example of this failure recently came to my attention. I was asked to see a woman who had been supporting her twenty-one-year-old daughter in a private institution at the cost of $550 a month for the preceding six and one-half years; the institution was now suggesting that the child go into a state hospital. This woman just could not accept the recommendation. In the course of our discussion it became increasingly clear that her daughter was dyslexic and that this had been unrecognized by one of the best institutions in this country. This is a shocking, sickening situation. Imagine how that young lady must feel to have spent six years in a place in which she did not belong!

Her plight is a combination of the impact of adolescence and the queer, confused, uncommunicative state of the perceptually handicapped. For a long while many people thought that these people had no feelings. The problem has been ours, not theirs. They have feelings just as exquisitely sensitive as ours, but the problem is the communication barrier. For many years I used to refer to myself as a worry-doctor to children. I was delighted one day when a child said to me, "You are my listening doctor." The problem we have with these children is to listen to the confusion of their emotions. Their problems with thought, with learning, and with behavior are recognized most of the time. They are talked about time and time again. It is true that they need to be emphasized, but they are now at least in front of our public attention. The feelings, however, are often forgotten. I now define psychiatry as the specialty of feelings. This is the area in which we need to move. The sensations, the desires, and the emotions of children are too often ignored or forgotten.

A T THE ANNUAL CONFERENCE of the Association for Children with Learning Disabilities, which was held in Boston in 1968, there was a panel that was comprised of adolescent perceptually handicapped children. Their own comments communicate to us the emotional aspect of their problems. The following are some of their contributions:

"I got the clowning but what I really wanted was respect and friendship."

"I want to grow up to be a man, but how can I?"

"My parents had me tested, said I was okay, figured I had it upstairs so then they felt I was lazy."

"No way out but cheating."

"I told the teacher I had kidney trouble, went to the john, looked up the answer."

"Athletics was a blessing. I felt it was one place where you could kill the teacher and it was legal."

"I really gave up in first grade. The more people shouted, the dumber I got."

Similarly, the following contributions were overheard in a classroom for learning disability adolescents:

"Tom, your handwriting is a little hard to read. Well, the kids who check my words are getting used to it. *That may be, but it is hard on your teacher to know what you mean.* Well, aren't you learning too?"

"Can I go to my books and get my locker? *No, I mean — no, the rule is you can't. But no one says you can't go to your books for a locker.* But I don't want my locker."

"I've got lots of problems. My mother and I are fighting. We had a disrespect fight. She said I asked her to forgive me too many times."

In answer to his peers who nominated him for room recording secretary, Mike

said, "You know I can't read or write
very fast. I will be glad to be nominated
for something else — like watering the
plants."

These comments convey the fact that feelings are there. We very
often don't get the opportunity to get inside the skin of these children.
They are the ones who have been able to communicate even though
their language is sometimes a little offbeat. But what about the children who can not communicate? What about the children with whom
there is only the possibility of guessing about their feelings? Consider the predicament that I once had when I was asked to do psychiatric treatment with a deaf mute. There was, at first, no apparent
means of communication. I do not know quite how we both came out
in that endeavor, but I certainly learned a lot. I learned that communication can be accomplished with such a person by writing on pads
of paper and even by making mud pies, such as is done with little
children, even though this was an older person. I learned that feelings are there, behind the "deaf and dumb" exterior.

Figure 1 provides a pertinent example of a child's description
of himself. This is a child in junior high school who has written his
own statement of his feelings.

Figure 1

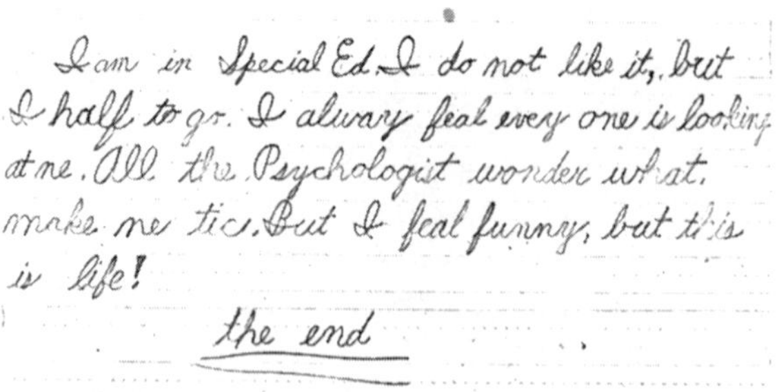

I am in Special Ed. I do not like it, but
I half to go. I alwary feal every one is looking
at me. All the Psychologist wonder what.
make me tic. But I feal funny, but this
is life!

the end

Who is to know his deeper feelings? This boy has described his
feelings superficially. I'm intrigued by the fact that he writes "the
end." This would be expected in a six-year-old or a seven-your-old.

Is this an example of his "leftover" immaturity, or is this child really saying, "I'm so depressed, this is the end"? These are the kinds of questions that need to be pursued.

Even more poignant to me, because I learned so much from the experience, was my interchange with John, a fourteen-year-old boy. He had been referred as a schizophrenic. He walked in like a robot; he practically clicked his heels. His speech was clipped; he sat down as if someone had turned a key. His facial expression was unrevealing; his answers went something like this: When I said to him, "How are you today?" he said, "Oh yes, how am I? You asked me how am I, yes I am fine." Silence. When I asked him if he could tell me a little about school, he said, "Oh how, what do I do in school? You asked what do I do in school? What do I do in school?" This kind of conversation for forty-five minutes leaves one a little bit frustrated. At the end of about twenty minutes, I asked him if he could draw a picture; he willingly said "Yes," and he drew a picture of the family (see *Figure 2*). One can sense the feeling in his drawings. He drew his father with hunched schoulders, hands unavailable; the mother is illustrated with a purse in her hand, again with a sort of unrelated

Figure 2

feeling to her shoulders and her arms; the cat is in between, and of course John is absent. When I asked him where he was, he said, "Lunch." Now that's funny, but it's also filled with pathos. He was fortunate enough to get the proper kind of education for a child with language problems, and the following examples of other drawings by

Figure 3

Figure 4

Figure 5

John give us indications of the nature of his feelings. The drawing in *Figure 3* is filled with good, healthy aggression. No schizophrenic child could ever reveal that. Aggression would be evidenced in a schizophrenic child, but it would not be so revealed. This shows two soldiers in close foreground, two in the distance; the spatial perception is excellent, the action clear. *Figure 4* shows a feudal battle. Again there is the bayoneted figure in the foreground. In *Figure 5*, John has drawn what could be Vesuvius exploding. This is a part of a much fuller drawing that was done in color, an exciting drawing.

Figure 6 shows tiny figures with much action. There are many different kinds of poses; the diagnosis of schizophrenia obviously does not fit

Figure 7

Figure 6

Figure 8

with this. In *Figure 7* John has drawn a frigate. He couldn't talk about this interest, but there it is on paper. Finally, *Figure 8* is an example of one of John's French lessons, in which he was asked to give the word translated from the English, and he added the very colorful, artistic touch.

THERE IS NO EDUCATION, no learning without emotion. There is similarly no child without emotion. The problem is communication. The perceptually handicapped child is truly multiply handicapped.

He has an ego deficit, and he has an emotional handicap. As far as I am concerned, every adolescent with a learning disability has a psychiatric problem as well.

The state of Illinois recently celebrated its 150th anniversary. At that time I was reminded of the epitaph on the tombstone of Abraham Lincoln's beloved Ann Rutledge: "Wedded to him not through union but through separation." I am very afraid that our devotion to many of these children is a romance similar to this; we are all too often wedded to these children, not through union but through separation. Perhaps refining our focus to the feelings of the adolescent, whatever his academic skills, will foster a more active union. I would hope so.

NOTES

1. Macdonald Critchley, *Developmental Dyslexia* (Springfield, Ill.: Charles C Thomas, 1964), p. 72.

How Do We Teach Him?

Laura E. Lehtinen-Rogan, Ph.D.

WE ALL KNOW CHILDREN who *don't* achieve well. However, there are also children who *can't* achieve well. Both the "don't achievers" and the "can't achievers" need help and understanding, but it is usually of a different kind. Unfortunately, both are often thought of as "won't achievers," and parents and teachers are prone to say, "He could do it if he would only try," or a variation on this theme, "He could do it if he would only try harder."

Upper-grade teachers are concerned in a somewhat different way with the child's development than are the primary- or early elementary-grade teachers. Teachers of adolescents are mainly concerned with the refinement of skills and their application to new learning or creative efforts, and they obviously do not have the time or special knowledge to develop foundation competencies, which should have been established in these children years before.

College teachers are in a somewhat better position. A system of prerequisites exists to insure that a student electing a particular course or course sequence has had at least some of the background the professor feels is necessary to derive full benefit from the course. A child enters a specific upper-grade class because he is fourteen years old and has been in school eight or nine years and because, for example, social studies is a requirement for graduation. Has he the prerequisites? Statistics are lacking, but experience suggests that as many as two or more children in a group of average size may be so deficient in the basic skills as to be seriously limited in their ability to participate in the class.

Achievement test scores do not always accurately reflect the academic retardation. Tests are designed to be used with a particular age range — grades four, five, and six or grades seven and eight, etc. A child answering a very few questions right, even if largely by chance, will be credited with the lowest scores that can be attained on the test. In actual fact, a child's functional skill in the area being tested may be considerably lower than suggested by the test score. The reverse may also be true. The test may underestimate the child's knowledge and concepts in such areas as social studies or arithmetic problem solving because of his inaccurate reading.

What are some of the reasons children don't achieve well? There is the child with gaps in his knowledge, which may necessitate tutoring at a particular time. The gaps may have come about through his absence when a particular phase of a skill was being developed, or through inefficient or inexperienced teaching, or other unfortunate circumstances. This child usually responds quickly and well to special help.

Everyone is familiar with the bright or even average child who is poorly motivated for academic learning and fails to make the effort to obtain good grades, or who cannot involve himself with the intensity and persistence that learning demands. These children often discover their interests and abilities much later in life. Some have emotional conflicts that interfere with learning, and they respond well in the classroom when helped through psychotherapy.

I should also like to comment on individual differences, a concept that has almost been forgotten. The structure of intelligence is so complex and many of its components apparently sufficiently independent of each other that unevenness of abilities in a person should be the rule rather than the exception. Few people can excel in all areas and few are without some areas of excellence. Many adults report that they were never very good in math, or sports, or music, or spatial orientation. These are persons who nevertheless may have completed college and are successful or even distinguished in professions that do not require a high level of skill in the areas in which they have lesser ability. Should these people be defined as having disabilities because of the discrepancy between their talents and weaker abilities? I should like to urge caution in defining special learning disabilities and, if possible, in separating individual *differences* from *disabilities*.

The three types of children just mentioned — the ones who missed out on certain learnings, or whose motivation is poor, or who may have much greater aptitude in certain areas than in others — are not the perceptually handicapped children being discussed in this paper, although they may well be in need of special educational help.

THE CHILDREN WITH special learning disabilities — perceptually handicapped children — are the ones who can't achieve well without special help and understanding. They seem to be troubled by much slower maturation rates or actual limitations in certain areas of function that are essential in learning fundamental literacy skills or in performing other mental operations ordinarily expected in the course of scholastic activity. The basis for the maldevelopment is not always clear. It may be related to "immaturity," that is, slow maturation of the central nervous system, which produces a lag in the development of some abilities. It may be the result of minimal brain damage occurring early in the child's life, which may not have reduced the child's intelligence significantly but which certainly interferes with its expression. It may be on the basis of a genetic factor, which is as yet not well understood but which is documented in many studies, particularly from England and the Scandinavian countries.

Studies in child development and psychological testing offer some guidelines to the maturation schedule of various mental abilities, but much more work in this area needs to be done. Studies of early childhood are more extensive than those dealing with later childhood or adolescence (due largely to the work of such pioneers as Jean Piaget and Arnold Gesell). It is known that there is a sequence in which such skills as finger prehension, visuo-motor perception, and speech sounds develop through neural maturation interacting with the ordinary stimulation of the environment. Teaching is most effective if it rides with the normal maturational advance, and frustrating and time wasting if it does not. Lauretta Bender has stated that various visuo-motor skills reach maturity at different ages, ranging up to about ten years of age, and Joseph Wepman tells us that the ability to discriminate differences in very similar speech sounds normally should be mature by the end of the eighth year. The child whose time table of maturation in any of these areas is paced at a slower tempo is certainly disadvantaged when competing with age contemporaries who grow at a faster maturation rate.

Parents are familiar with this phenomenon through their children's efforts to learn to ride a two-wheeler. Very often the child will wish to relinquish his training wheels but is not yet able to manage the coordination of balance required to ride without them. After a winter of no practice, during which the bike has been stored in the basement, the child takes it out in the spring and rides with no further practice or instruction. The winter has been a time of maturing for the central nervous system so that when presented with the specific demands of maintaining balance on two moving wheels, it is adequate to the demand. Much practice during the preceding summer would have been unrewarding both to parent and child, and could have established attitudes about self and the bike that would hinder later efforts at a more propitious time. An analogous situation applies in other areas of learning. Stimulation or specific practice is beneficial when the underlying base is adequately mature.

In working with the older child with learning problems, it is assumed that he has passed the age when the functions associated with a particular aspect of learning should normally have matured, yet testing indicates the level of certain skills to be still below age expectancy. If factors of opportunity and motivation are excluded, there may be justification for thinking in terms of a severe lag in maturation, or a dysfunction on a genetic or neurological basis. It is not known how long in a child's life maturation in some of these areas goes on. It is known that he can and does continue to learn. Some of us feel that he develops compensatory ways of meeting demands requiring the use of his lagging or underdeveloped abilities.

Those who speak and write about these children are often criticized for giving fine descriptions of their behavior, but few prescriptions. The experienced observers — teachers and others who work with these children — can also describe with accuracy the various behaviors. The justification for giving such descriptions here, perhaps, is to help others confirm their own observations, and to increase their understanding of the child as a person with problems in learning. From this understanding, original ideas may flow for improving the child's condition.

BEHAVIOR

By the time a child with learning disabilities related to minimal brain dysfunction reaches the junior high school or high school level, many of the more obvious distinguishing features he may have had as a younger child have smoothed out and become less noticeable, if not less troublesome. This is due to the combined effect of the physiological maturation that has been going on, helping his central nervous system "catch up" somewhat, and to the learning that has occurred both about the kinds of behaviors that are acceptable and the kinds that are not, as well as about various compensations he may need to make in order to get along.

Consequently, much of the characteristic symptomatology is going on *inside* the child, in relation to the lesson he should be understanding or the work he should be producing. It is more subtle and harder to observe than in the younger child and, of course, is masked by many attitudes and disguises the child may have adopted along the way. In years to come, it may be possible to relate many of these characteristics to some general function with a scholarly name such as "integrative activity of the nervous system," but for the present, descriptions of observable behavior, such as the following, are the best approach.

Distractibility

Even the older, perceptually handicapped child still finds it difficult to tune out external or internal stimulation under certain circumstances. In class, movements of other children and outdoor noises may be sufficiently intrusive to interfere with concentration. I remember a younger child (then eleven years of age) who angrily closed the window on a particularly lovely spring day and stormed at a bird on a nearby branch. The bird's rhapsodizing was creating an intolerable distraction. For this type of child, a study hall with large numbers of children is a place to endure rather than one in which to get work done.

Inability to Sustain Attention

Often these children have developed the capacity to focus attention for short periods of time but cannot sustain it. They stop listening in class, perhaps to daydream or, in consequence of being distracted, perhaps simply because their mechanism shuts off – it has had enough. It cannot take in and process more at this time. After a while it will be fresh and ready to go again. This tendency is a handicap in the group instructional situation as well as in doing independent work. I remember one child who would tell his teacher when he felt his tolerance level approaching, "Don't show me anything more about this today.

I think I've got it and if you tell me anything else I'm afraid I'll get mixed up." He was able to speak openly to his teacher, but picture the child in class who must appear to be listening and understanding, yet for whom the instruction becomes only a flow of words after his point of tolerance has been exceeded.

Breaks in Continuity of Thought

Intrusions from the outside or extraneous material from their own thoughts erupt into the listening or producing process. Sometimes this amounts to no more than an interruption in the stream of thought; sometimes it is seen as an interruption of an irrelevant idea introduced into a discussion.

Characteristics such as these have a profound effect on the child's ability to obtain information, regardless of whether the input is through listening or reading, since much of the time he is not adequately tuned in. They also affect his ability to produce, for example, homework assignments and reports. Time is finite. A certain portion of the adolescent child's time, whether he has a learning disability or not, is taken up with the business of living — eating, traveling about, washing, shopping, along with some sports and social activities. It may take the child who is inefficient about concentrating, who is easily distracted, or who has, as they used to be called, "poor work habits," twice as long to cover the same amount of material as the good student. A conscientious child with a learning disability may spend hours at his homework to the exclusion of other important but not so high-priority activities.

Poor Feedback

All of our activities are accompanied by a constant process of monitoring their quality and accuracy. As an act is in process, the individual's monitoring system (or feedback system) is tuned in to the act, ready to revise, correct, change intensity or whatever else his perception of the act informs him is necessary. If one's voice is too loud, he moderates it; if his pencil pressure is too light, he presses harder; if he misspeaks a word, he hears it and corrects himself. Many children with perceptual problems do not monitor their performances efficiently. This is very apparent in spelling; the child does not perceive at the same time all the many aspects of the process and so does not "notice" the mistakes he makes as he writes the words. This same child may do much better on his weekly spelling tests, in which he simply needs to perceive the correctness of the dictated word and not the many other aspects of the total writing process.

Overlooking or Not Noticing

Many perceptually handicapped children will fail to note an item in their work that they are quite capable of doing, as though for the moment the intake mechanism were shut off. We all do this to some degree, I might add, when we cannot "see" something we are looking for. Children turn in pages on which one or two problems are omitted and then respond with great surprise when this is called to their attention. These children do part of an arithmetic problem and leave the remainder unfinished, going on to the next, without "noticing."

Poor Organization

Children with problems in spatial organization very often experience difficulty organizing and arranging material on a page. Words are sprinkled about rather than being written in columns; various steps of a problem are scattered hither and yon. They seem not to have learned some of the most elemental aspects of organization such as centering a title, leaving a space between lines, and keeping a margin. The notebooks of these children are similarly disorganized. The ones with problems of left-right organization (laterality) will write with the holes on the right side of the paper and then be chagrined when the paper must be placed in the book upside down.

Quite obviously, problems like these result in poor quality on tests and homework assignments and very often the judgment of "carelessness" on the part of teachers and parents. Organization of papers can be improved by a teacher who sets standards and requires that the child be attentive to these matters. The "overlooking" or "not noticing" is harder to change. A child can be encouraged to proofread his material, but even this will not always be effective since he reads the errors as though they were not there and the omissions as though they were. Nevertheless, it is worth a try, despite the additional time it takes from his already overfilled schedule.

Difficulty in Selecting

Many of these children have problems in deciding on that which is significant, relevant, and important. They may extract details rather than the main ideas from their reading, and have difficulty summarizing and reporting. This may reflect a looseness in thinking wherein all ideas are equally relevant and interesting, or it may reflect problems in abstract thinking.

Lack of Resourcefulness

This might be called lack of flexibility, lack of imagination, inability to see other possible solutions to a difficulty, or possibly acceptance of inferior quality because this is the way it has always been and is all that the individual has ever known. Perhaps the most familiar difficulty in this area is the child's inability to solve an arithmetic problem because he can't restructure it in terms that are familiar to him and that are normally more accessible to solution. I have been impressed with the answer of children who have spelling difficulties when they are asked how they study their spelling words. It is not uncommon for the child to say, ''I look at them.'' This obviously is the technique the child has used all along. He applies it without adjusting to the nature of the material and without having discovered a way that would result in greater success for him. Other children – poor readers – when asked what they do about words they don't know will say, ''I skip them,'' or ''I guess.'' Sometimes this technique is helpful but only if it can be used in combination with other helps. Children with poor writing quality will make no effort to adjust the position of the paper but will continue to write even as their arm and hand are falling off the desk. Some children can only guess or count if they do not know arithmetic combinations. They have not learned to ''think around'' the problem – to use knowledge that they already possess.

Resourcefulness is a creative, integrative capacity insofar as it enables an individual to apply previously learned skills or knowledge in an adaptive way to a new situation. Perhaps the resourceful, creative, perceptually handicapped children are the ones who discover their own methods of compensation, even though these may often appear to be devious and inefficient to their elders.

Deficient Memory

Underlying all of the child's learning activities is memory of one kind or another, which enables him to accumulate, store, and make available past information. This is a capacity in which many, but not necessarily all, perceptually handicapped children are deficient and in which some children are selectively deficient to the irritation of their teachers and parents. Memory is not a unitary mental ability. There are several identifiable kinds. It is quite possible for a child (particularly the one with a severe reading disability) to have a rather good memory for events and experiences in his life but to have great difficulty remembering rather arbitrary, rote learnings such as the alphabet or multiplication tables. His failure with the latter is usually attributed to disinterest, lack of effort, or poor motivation. Undoubtedly his low motivation has much to do with it, but he has learned from his own experience not to expect too much success with such memory exercises. Earlier successes would have created an expectation of mastery and consequently greater drive to accomplish what may be an intrinsically uninteresting task.

This list of characteristics and examples is by no means exhaustive, as any who have worked with perceptually handicapped children know only too well. I have tried to select some of the most common ones to point up the kinds of problems teachers of adolescents would be most apt to encounter.

THE LIST OF PROBLEMS is not at an end, however. Any teacher, but more so the teacher of older children, must contend with all of the past learnings of the child. It is naturally enormously discouraging to the upper-grades teacher to receive a piece of written work with 20 percent of the words misspelled, with incomplete sentences, poorly punctuated if at all, and written in a barely legible hand with many erasures and crossed out words. It is all the more depressing to reflect that this may be an example of the child's skills in such other areas as reading and arithmetic as well.

In such a case, much of the problem may be seen at a glance. He has *not* learned or mastered skills that he should now have. He has confused things that have been taught so that he is not sure of how and why he must perform certain operations. He may have actual misinformation — wrongly perceived, misunderstood but well retained. From his paper, the compensations he has tried to make and the inefficient procedures he has adopted, cannot be seen. His work habits and some attitudes may be reflected in the standard he sets for himself. One can only guess at the feelings he has. It is well to remember that the perceptually handicapped child is experiencing the effects of a chronic condition, which has been with him from birth or a very early age. He does not know anything else. He cannot know what it is like to be different; he has never experienced it. He cannot know how other children think or learn because he has only his own experience to look back on.

What ray of light is there in this picture of gloom? There are at least two. Earlier I commented on the physiological growth that occurs in the child's nervous system. The gradual maturation of the neural system, even though slower than in a nonhandicapped child, may have brought certain perceptual abilities to a level where they can now be used for specific learnings. A child with considerable auditory discrimination difficulty at the age of eight or nine may no longer have that degree of difficulty at thirteen. As a result, he can now respond to phonics instruction because one of the basic abilities has reached its full maturation. A similar process is going on in the visual modality, and things that were confusing and difficult earlier, now seem better structured and organized.

A second plus for the child is the social-emotional maturation of attitudes that may have occurred, provided no serious emotional disturbances are present. Many children, not only perceptually handicapped children, get off to a poor start in school because they are socially (or emotionally) a little too immature to grasp the significance of the experience they are involved in. They are not aware of the grave consequences that ensue if this great game of going to school is not played according to the rules or with full participation. Even children with considerable learning difficulty are able to reflect on their earlier behavior, evaluating it quite adequately. "I used to play around a lot when I was in second grade," or "I didn't like my third-grade teacher and I didn't do any work that year," are not necessarily excuses the child is inventing to explain his scholastic retardation; he is also reporting the situation as he remembers it and as, to some extent at least, it actually existed. With greater social-emotional maturity he is better equipped to appreciate the necessity for self-discipline in learning, responsibility for meeting deadlines, sacrificing some of his pleasures for work, and so on.

If the teacher finds that he can work with the child and can elicit his cooperation, it will not be distorting the truth to tell him that because he is older, some of the things he found difficult as a younger child are worth trying again as they will now not be as hard to learn.

On the other hand, the child is not conscious that he is developing new mental competencies unless he has an opportunity to experience the change. He needs suggestions as to new ways of doing old things — and a chance to experiment with them. Very important, however, is a feeling of freedom to experiment, even if the results are not always the best. In most group or classroom situations the penalty is too high, the risk too great. If his effort doesn't work, his grades drop and the quality of his work falls. His functioning is too marginal to allow anything except what he knows from past experience will work, regardless of its inefficiency. By reducing the emotional risks of poor performance, the teacher may be developing greater resourcefulness and the courage to experiment and try new approaches.

METHODS FOR THE CLASSROOM

This rather extensive prologue has been presented to help develop a context of understanding, within which the following suggestions for the classroom teacher may be meaningful.

1. A very good way to assess the level of a group of students is to begin the year with an original essay or composition to be written during classtime. From the results, the teacher can easily identify the child with poor spelling, handwriting problems, a poor background in punctuation and sentence construction, immature expression, limited or bizarre fantasy, poor organization of his thoughts, and many other characteristics. This is a very effective screening device that can yield a gold mine of information. Don't expect gold, however, and don't wilt from discouragement at what is found.

2. The teacher should let the child whose effort is obviously poor know that he is interested in the child and that he is willing to help to the extent that his time and knowledge allows. In most instances, the child will receive the offer with inner relief, if not outward expression.

3. Standards and expectations are important for the child with a learning problem no less so than for the average learner. If a feeble

effort is accepted, all but the highly motivated, ambitious children will turn in a feeble effort. We all know that all of us can be pressed to greater efforts than we normally produce. However, the most meaningful expectations are expressed as specific standards. It is not only not helpful, it is demoralizing to a child to receive a paper on which the teacher has given him a failing grade with a comment about "sloppy work, I can't read it." This is the "straighten out and shape up" attitude which puts the burden entirely on the child. In addition, it cuts deep into already sensitive feelings. It is entirely reasonable to state that papers should be written in ink or pencil, with a margin line drawn on them, with a space between paragraphs, with attention to capitals, spelling, and legible writing. If the perceptually handicapped child has even a modicum of skills, he will try to meet expectations that have been clearly stated, and he will do so with pride. The teacher must be aware, however, that it may be extremely difficult, if not actually impossible, for some perceptually handicapped children to turn in a piece of written work with no technical errors. The page that is turned in, even with errors, may represent a third or fourth copy. If the quality of the work is still very inferior or does not reflect much thought or effort, the teacher might write "See me" on the paper and go over specific points like those mentioned.

4. The teacher should take time to study the child's record. The school will often have considerable information on the child's abilities, achievements, disabilities, and personality. This effort can save time. It may also provide helpful insights into the effectiveness of past attempts to help the child.

5. Ten or fifteen minutes a day should be utilized, if possible, to go over a few points individually with the perceptually handicapped pupil. Certainly in this amount of time the teacher cannot correct very many of the child's problems, but he can often help a great deal to undo some long-standing confusions that will get the child going again. The following suggestions may prove helpful for the teacher who is able to schedule individual help for the child:

• Encourage him to ask questions about points he did not understand, but do not be surprised by their quality. They may often impress you as trifling and minor points, but they are of importance to the pupil since he is bringing them up as barriers to understanding. His long background of experience may have taught him to be wary of asking publicly in order to shield himself from the scorn of his peers. Or he may have discovered that teachers are impatient with a simple question and that they answer it by repeating an explanation rather than making a real effort to develop an explanation that would clarify. It is also possible that, lacking practice, he doesn't know how to ask a question well. I assure you that you will be amazed at the kinds of questions that will come up. At the Cove Schools we maintain the attitude that no problem is too small and that regardless of how minor it may seem to be, it deserves sincere and respectful consideration.

• Being aware that the perceptually handicapped child may have missed out on some specific items of information, question him (tactfully but directly) on them. Find out whether he knows what an antonym or an adjective is. Ask him whether he can tell the difference between an adverb and an adjective, if he knows how to read decimals, or if he really knows what is meant by an angle (is it the length of the lines or the distance between?), etc. Your personal effort to clarify some of these small but basic points may yield good results. Keep a small notebook to jog your memory on the need for specific work pages or review.

• If you are teaching new material, remember that the perceptually handicapped pupil may grasp only a part of the lesson from your group explanation because of his easy distractibility or inability to sustain attention for long. You can go over some of the lesson again with him individually, giving him the benefit of hearing it twice and of asking questions. Let him take a copy of of the book home to reread.

• The perceptually handicapped child may have difficulty understanding some of the concepts you are presenting. Relating these to his own experiences or to other concepts taught earlier will often help him. A child without problems will do this spontaneously — the perceptually handicapped child needs leading.

• Usually he needs more practice to thoroughly establish a particular skill. Extra papers torn from a workbook or a ditto sheet covering a special process assigned as a study hall or a homework aid may give him the extra practice he needs, without being burdensome.

- Make it a habit to ask him to tell you the important points of the lesson, or go through a process step by step to check on his understanding of it. If he can tell it to you, he probably understands it and will retain most of it.

- Many perceptually handicapped children wander away from the topic in their interest to report details. They find it hard to summarize or to select the most important thought from the reading material. In individual sessions you can gradually help them become more selective and to group ideas a little better.

- Some perceptually handicapped children need a little more time to think. Pressure causes them to block, but if you can wait just a trifle longer than ordinarily, they often can come up with the answer. Also, if the child realizes that you will give him time to think and not just hustle him along, he will be better able to respond.

- The anxiety of not knowing the answer (on tests or in written work) may result in a defeatist attitude with very low output. Some children can be encouraged to skip a problem or a question and return to it after the disorganizing emotion has subsided.

- Review, review, review. Pick up important points frequently and quiz the child on his mastery. Many perceptually handicapped children don't retain well. They need to "over-learn" material until it stays with them.

6. The child with seriously deficient skills in reading, spelling and handwriting presents special problems. If he is recovering from a long-standing reading disability, his skill or speed may not yet be totally adequate for the reading load of the secondary school. It would seem reasonable for a child like this to have someone, a parent or a senior-citizen volunteer, read some of his material to him while his skills are in the process of improving. One of my colleagues recently made the suggestion that talking books for the blind might help to fill this need for the poor reader.

A similar situation is presented by the child with poor manual dexterity and resulting poor handwriting skill. Some children have learned to write acceptably well, but so slowly that they cannot keep up with the class. I would like to see an effort made to teach typing skills at an earlier age level, again possibly through the help of volunteers. In some instances a parent or another child may serve as secretary. At times, just giving the child as much time as he needs will be enough, but this may mean that the teacher might need to schedule a second session of work with him or permit him to finish an assignment at home.

At this point, the following question is pertinent: "Won't the child become so comfortable with these arrangements that he will want to continue them indefinitely and not strive to achieve these skills through his own efforts?" This may indeed be a possibility, but a serious one only for the child who already has dependency problems. A child whose personality development is reasonably healthy will want to give up his dependence on a parent or teacher or volunteer at the earliest possible opportunity unless he has been taught to believe that he is incompetent and incapable of functioning without such help. The goal of doing it alone as other children do is what he would also like to achieve.

Some children may even be willing to practice to improve the quality of their handwriting if it is a specific assignment. Poor handwriting due to motor incoordination cannot be greatly improved. Much poor handwriting, however, is due to carelessness, excessive haste, mixing up cursive and printed forms, and to writing too small. The assignment may be no more complicated than carefully copying a short paragraph from the text that is ordinarily used by the class.

What can be done with the child who can't spell? First, I'd like to suggest that the teacher grade his papers twice, the first time for content and the second time for spelling. If he wishes, the two may be averaged into a total grade. Then, in individual sessions, the child should be helped to make an active effort to improve his spelling. The teacher may suggest techniques to the child, like saying the names of the letters in the word over and over until he knows them by heart, trying to visualize how the word looks, writing it and comparing it with the model, finding a funny way to remember, as by pronouncing the silent letters ("knee" as "k-nee") or discovering that there is a *rat* in *separate*. It is, of course, important to elicit the child's cooperation in such a venture, and the teacher's objectives should be discussed with the child. This is another occasion when a volunteer can be helpful in drilling a child on his misspelled words.

Poor organization of materials on a page is a handicap that is almost as troublesome as poor spelling. This will yield if the child's need for improvement is discussed with him, if he is made aware that this is neither necessary nor acceptable, and if he is shown how to have his papers organized. He should be steered in the right direction and expected to follow the indicated path, not just turned loose to stumble along by himself.

7. What about the problem of tests and examinations? It is superfluous to mention that the perceptually handicapped child is penalized by all of the deficits I have discussed earlier. He reads the questions slowly and possibly inaccurately; he writes slowly, spells poorly, organizes his page badly, and yet he may have acceptable understanding of the material and command of the facts presented. It would seem only fair for him to have the opportunity to be tested separately on his knowledge rather than on these more mechanical skills. Again, with a little imagination and some generosity of feeling, the teacher could test a child with these problems orally, or if this is not possible, permit him to dictate answers to a tape recorder or to a volunteer who will write them down. In past generations, the illiterate member of society paid a scribe to put his words and thoughts on paper because he lacked the education to do it himself. Our compulsory education plan has brought us to a point where some of our "illiterate" children are living in a literate school environment, but we do not admit to their need or provide them with the scribe that earlier cultures supplied.

8. What about homework? I know some conscientious perceptually handicapped children who spend literally hours at their homework to the exclusion of recreation and socialization. This may be because their tool skills are poor but also because their concentration and study habits are inefficient. If the teacher becomes aware of this, a lighter homework load or an understanding with some of the other teachers who also assign homework may be in order.

9. We hear a great deal about the place of reward in learning. Obviously, the teacher of the adolescent cannot deal out gold stars or candy or pats on the head. Rewards, or reinforcers, need to be more

subtle. A smile is tremendously rewarding to an unsure or discouraged child. When the teacher returns the child's paper, he should put several comments on it: "Spelling is improving." "Very neat this time." "Good sentences." Then he can add, "We need to work on organization." This often is helpful in stimulating the child to accomplish the task.

10. The following is so well known to teachers that it scarcely needs comment: A way must be found for this child to contribute something to the class, either individually or as a member of a subgroup. He needs to be encouraged to add to class discussions. Whatever other capabilities he may have, they should be exploited for this purpose. Success has a special sweetness to those who do not experience it often. This may not be helping to resolve his learning disability, but it will help him feel better about school and himself.

I have purposely not mentioned any of the more technical things that a teacher who has specialized in work with perceptually handicapped children might do. Instead I have wanted to indicate some of the things a nonspecialist can do if he has some understanding of the problems and some affection for the child. Teachers are skilled in making observations. When they add kindly interest and imagination to their observations, they will have the means for helping the perceptually handicapped child go a long way toward a more productive learning experience. The bright child teaches himself — he needs the teacher to lead the way and open doors. The child with learning disabilities needs the teacher to enlighten, clarify, organize, and support.

11. The child's classroom teacher should work with the resource teacher or the special learning disabilities teacher if he is fortunate enough to have one in his school. The specialist cannot do the job alone — he sees the child a few hours a week at the most. The education of the child with a learning disability must be seen as a shared responsibility, with all of the child's teachers making a team effort.

WHAT IS THE OUTLOOK for children with problems like these? Do any of them actually "make it"? The fact is that they do, and a large part of the credit for their success is due to the understanding and extra effort of observant teachers. I am acquainted with young adults who were perceptually handicapped children, who are now attending colleges, or who have graduated from universities, or who are now in graduate school. I know others for whom high school has been the last school experience and who are now working. I know others who have had to content themselves with more modest goals.

Several factors help to predict a child's attainments:

• One of the most important, obviously, is the level of general ability. All other things being equal, a bright child with perceptual handicaps or learning disabilities will be expected to progress further in school than a child with average or slow-learner abilities. It should be remembered, though, that the bright child, because of his brightness may be intensely troubled by what he senses is his dullness in learning. Maintaining a reasonably good self-concept is difficult in the face of daily defeats.

• A child with minimal or few handicaps can surmount their effect more easily than the child with multiple handicaps, even though these multiple handicaps are minor ones.

• A child who has the drive and the desire and the strong motivation to put in the long hours and intensive effort it often requires for him to be able to achieve, will do more than another child who has an easygoing nature.

• The child who is emotionally strong enough and mature enough to make a respected place for himself in the stream, even though the going is sometimes rough, can be counted on to come through.

Challenge is not new to teachers. There are just new challenges. The efforts of teachers and educators to understand the problem of the child with learning disabilities brings us close to the very core of how learning itself occurs. This is one of the most exciting challenges of all.

About the Authors

CHARLES R. STROTHER, PH.D., is professor of psychology and clinical psychology in medicine at University of Washington, Seattle.

ROSA A. HAGIN, PH.D., is assistant professor in clinical psychology at New York University School of Medicine, New York.

MARY GIFFIN, M.D., is medical director of the North Shore Mental Health Association and The Irene Josselyn Clinic, Northfield, Illinois.

LAURA E. LEHTINEN-ROGAN, PH.D., is clinical director of The Cove Schools, Evanston, Illinois, and Racine, Wisconsin.